Stories About God's Goodness

A Personal Testimony

Betty Ann and Gary Phillips

This book is dedicated to our two sons, their wives, and our four grandchildren. May you always tell your God stories!

Stories About God's Goodness
A Personal Testimony

By Betty Ann and Gary Phillips

Contents

GOD IS GOOD!

Many of you have seen the movie, "God's Not Dead," and remember the lines two pastors lightly said to each other when things were not going well—"God is good all the time" and "All the time, God is good." Actually, these simple words proclaim the powerful truth that our God is in fact good. This truth is clearly stated in Psalm 34:8 which says, *"Taste and see that the Lord is good,"* and in Psalm 107:1 which says, *"Give thanks to the Lord, for he is good; his love endures forever."*

As you read the Bible, you find that it is filled with wonderful stories that illustrate God's goodness. For example, Exodus 16 tells the miraculous story of God providing manna from heaven to feed the Israelites wandering in the desert. Also, John 9 describes the miracle of Jesus healing a man who was born blind;

Psalm 34 tells of God delivering David from all his fears; Daniel 6 describes God supernaturally protecting Daniel when he was in the den of lions; and 2 Chronicles 1 tells of God blessing Solomon with wisdom and knowledge.

What is really amazing is that this good, all-powerful God continues today to show us His goodness in so many ways. He cares about every aspect of our lives and desires to have an intimate relationship with us. As part of this, it is normal for Christians to regularly experience God's goodness through supernatural interactions and interventions in their lives.

This book contains my stories and testimonies of what a good and awesome God has done for me as I walked with Him over the years. God has no favorites and I am just an ordinary woman saved by the grace of God. Thus, the stories of God's goodness that I share are not unique to me and, as you think over your past, most likely you can remember times that God moved supernaturally in your life. My hope in writing this book is that God is glorified and lifted up, His goodness becomes more real to you, and you live with a greater expectancy that God is ready to intervene in your life with provision, healing, deliverance, and blessings.

STORIES ABOUT GOD'S FINANCIAL PROVISION

One of the best-known names of God is Jehovah Jireh, which means God our Provider. We should find comfort in this because as humans we have many basic needs such as food, shelter, clothes, jobs, and money. All too often we focus on our needs instead of on God, our provider, who meets these needs. In Matthew 6:26, Jesus says, *"Look at the birds of the air; they do not sow or reap or store away in barns, and yet your heavenly Father feeds them. Are you not much more valuable than they?"* Christians should walk with the assurance that God will provide for their needs. David said in Psalm 37:25, *"I was young and now I am old, yet I have never seen the righteous forsaken or their children begging bread."*

My husband and I have been married for over 50 years and during this time God has always provided for our financial needs. God blessed my husband with a wonderful career and today we have a nice home and live comfortably. But, things were far different during the early years of our marriage when my husband was in college. Like many families just getting started, we had little and were financially very poor.

About two years after we were married, our financial situation got even worse. I became pregnant with our first son and early in the pregnancy, I began to have some problems. My doctor said that our baby was at risk and that I needed to quit my job so I could stay off my feet. My husband was still in college and, after I stopped working, his part-time job became our only source of income. One week during this time we had only $2.00 between us and still had several days before my husband's next payday. I was so upset. Our refrigerator and cupboard were practically empty and my husband needed gas so he could drive to his classes and to his part-time job. I prayed and cried out to God for help! Soon after I prayed, my father showed up at our front door. He was carrying two bags full of groceries! I had not said a word to my father about needing anything, yet there he was! The next day my husband's parents came over for a visit. When they left, they gave us $25.00! With these blessings, I was beginning to learn that God truly is our provider.

A couple of months after I quit my job, I was better and able to get out of the house. But, I had no maternity clothes. I told my husband that I needed some undergarments and maternity dresses. He handed me $9.00 and said that was all we could possibly spare for clothing. Well, $9.00 was very little money even in 1970! I looked at the small sum of money and then I looked to God. I prayed and asked God to direct me to where I should go to find clothing. I got into our car and began driving. All of a sudden the name of a store popped into my head and I drove there. I looked for undergarments first because that was what I needed most. To my surprise and excitement, the store had just what I needed for only $3.00!

I thanked the Lord and asked Him where I should go to get maternity dresses with only $6.00 left to my name. This task seemed impossible, but I was so encouraged by God's provision regarding the undergarments. Another store's name came to mind and I began driving there. When I arrived, the store had women's summer shifts on sale for only $2.00. I was so excited because the shifts would work perfectly as maternity dresses. I actually got three dresses for only $6.00—what a way to shop! With God's direction, I went to only two stores and obtained everything I needed for exactly the small amount of money that I had. What a good God we serve!

A few months later I delivered a healthy baby boy. When he was about one year old, I wanted to purchase a small plastic wading pool for him to be able to play in during the summer. Money was still very tight and my husband said we could only spare $2.00 for a wading pool. Honestly, I was not optimistic about finding a plastic pool for this price. But, I prayed that God would help and I began shopping. Once again, God put the name of a discount

7

department store in my mind and I drove there. When I walked to the section of the store that sold plastic pools, there was a large pile of small pools stacked on top of each other. I looked at the pools on top of the pile and none of them was even close to $2.00. I prayed and, by faith, I reached in towards the bottom of the pile and pulled out a pool. This one had a red sticker on it marked $1.89! God provided again and I was able to buy the wading pool for my son.

Whenever I needed something or wanted to buy something special for someone, I learned to pray about it and trust God to tell me where to go and when to go for the lowest price. For example, I wanted a rose-colored pair of slacks and prayed that God would let me know where and when to buy them. My husband and I were traveling and we stopped at a department store for some shopping. Upon entering the store, I went to the section where items were on sale. On a large rack of clothes, I saw two pairs of rose-colored slacks and when I looked, not one, but both were my size! God often multiplies the blessings and goes the second mile when we seek Him. By the way, the slacks originally sold for $54.00 but were on sale for only $7.00 dollars!

I want to be a good steward of the money God places in my hands, so even today, I never pay the original marked price for clothing. When I see a garment that I would like to have and it is not on sale, I pray and ask God to save it for me if that is in His will. I then wait until I feel the leading of the Lord to return to the store. Time after time the exact garment I wanted is still there but is now on the sale rack at a price that I feel comfortable with. God is so good and really cares about all the details in our life.

A few years after the wading pool purchase, God began teaching me about tithing and its relationship to blessings and provision. I read in Malachi chapter 3 that if you do not tithe, then you are robbing from God—something that I did not want to do! Also, Malachi 3:10 actually states that tithing is an area where God invites you to test Him. The scripture says, *"Test me in this, says the Lord Almighty, and see if I will not throw open the floodgates of heaven and pour out so much blessing that there will not be room enough to store it."* Well, I realized that everything we have is because of God's goodness and grace. I also realized that God could have asked for ninety, not ten, percent of our income as a tithe. But, He only asks for ten percent and even this is only to open the windows of heaven so that blessings fall to us. With this understanding, I began to trust what God said about tithing and I began to tithe whatever money came into my hands, including our weekly budget for groceries and gas. I did not tell my husband about this because at the time he was not yet walking with God and would not have understood.

Everything was going well until one day I felt that God asked me to give to Him half of our weekly budget for groceries and gas. In obedience to God, I gave half of our grocery and gas money to the church that week. I was happy because I obeyed God and we made it through the week without any noticeable problems. But then, in the following week, I felt that God asked me to give to Him not ten percent or even half of our grocery and gas money, but to give all of the money! This frightened me because my car was already running on fumes and I knew I had to drive that week and would need to buy gas. If I ran out of money, my husband would never understand what I had done. But, I trust God and wanted to be obedient. So, I gave all of our weekly grocery and gas money to the church that week without anyone knowing about it. I tried my best to conserve gas as much as possible, but I still had to drive for errands and to our children's school.

Near the end of the week, I knew I was out of gas—the gas gauge had been registering empty for a while. Then, my husband asked me to do something for him that required me to drive. I got into the car knowing I had no gas. I talked to God and gently reminded Him of my situation. By faith, I started the car and saw a miracle unfold right before my eyes! I actually watched the gas gauge begin moving! God was supernaturally filling up the car's gas tank! I was amazed at God's provision and blessing. He is truly Jehovah Jireh, God our provider.

Several years later when our younger son was about nine years old, the music teacher at his school called and said that my son wanted to learn to play the piano. I told the teacher that that was wonderful, but we did not have a piano for him to learn on. When my son came home from school, I talked to him about his desire and explained that pianos are expensive and we did not have enough extra money to purchase one. His response surprised me. He said that was okay because God would give him a piano for Christmas. Well, it was only two weeks before Christmas. I did not see how it was possible for us to find a piano in so little time and especially at a price we could afford. So he would not be disappointed, I tried to tell my son that this might not happen. But again, he looked at me and confidently said that God would give him a piano. Well, I really started praying and asking God to honor my son's faith. A week later we learned of someone who had a good used piano for sale. When we called, wonder of wonders the piano price was well below what it was worth and we were able to buy it! God answered my prayers, honored my son's faith, and provided a piano for Christmas! God is so good!

I have two more short stories that illustrate
God's goodness by being our provider. First,
as Christmas approached one year, I thought
that it would be nice if I could give each of my
sisters a nice robe for a present. My husband
and I were eating at a fast food restaurant a
few weeks before Christmas when I felt the
prompting of the Holy Spirit to go to one of the
better department stores in our area. We
quickly finished eating and drove to the store.
When we got to the appropriate section of the
store, we found a clerk who was in the process
of marking a rack of $80.00 robes down to
$10.00! The clerk said this was not an
advertised special but that the store manager
had just come by and told her to put the robes
on clearance sale. Because of God's
goodness, I was able to purchase very nice
robes for my sisters at a great bargain!

Second, during a break at a Christian conference I was attending, I decided to purchase a CD set at the conference's product table. I opened my purse to pay for the set and found that I did not have a credit card with me. The woman cashier at the table watched me as I searched and searched my purse looking for cash. I finally found enough money for the purchase—except for 75 cents. The woman saw my dilemma and said that she would pay the 75 cents and for me not to worry about it. I thanked her and picked up the CDs. When I got back to my seat, I told God that the woman did not know me and should not have to help pay for my purchase. I immediately felt prompted to look in my purse again. Even though I had thoroughly searched my purse just moments before, I now saw three new, shiny quarters! I was so excited that God had supernaturally put the quarters in my purse. It was a well-attended conference and I did not know where the woman was so I could repay

15

her. I asked God to let me find the woman and, as soon as I prayed, the speaker called on a woman in the audience to stand. It was the woman at the table who gave the money! As soon as the meeting was over, I went straight to her, thanked her again for her kindness, and gave her the three shiny quarters. God cared that I did not want to owe anyone and He provided. God is so faithful to us.

STORIES ABOUT GOD'S HEALING MIRACLES

Both the Old and New Testaments contain many stories of God's power and goodness exhibited through miraculous healings of the sick. Many of you have wonderful testimonies of God supernaturally healing someone in response to your prayers. At the same time, you may also have stories where it seemed that God did not answer prayers to heal the sick. We do not always understand why we see healing miracles in some cases but not in other cases. I believe that part of the answer lies in 1 Corinthians 13:12 which states, *"Now all we can see of God is like a cloudy picture in a mirror. Later we will see him face to face. We don't know everything, but then we will, just as God completely understands us."* (Contemporary English Version) What I do know is that God is always good and that we should always celebrate and praise Him. I am so thankful to God for the stories below that describe just a few of the healing miracles that I have personally seen in my family.

After we were married, I noticed that my husband used a lot of nasal decongestant spray. When I asked about it, he said that for several years he had used the spray to relieve nasal congestion so he could breathe through his nose rather than his mouth. He actually had gone through an unsuccessful surgery to correct the problem. His doctor had recommended another surgery, but my husband did not want to go through that again. So, several times a day he would use the spray. Part of the problem was that although the spray worked for a while, it also resulted in a rebound reaction that would cause swelling and the congestion to return. It was a vicious cycle that he was unable to break. Obviously, I felt sorry for my husband and I began to ask God to heal him of this problem.

Before going to bed each night, I prayed and, if I woke up during the night, I would lay my hand on him and pray again. I remembered the scripture in Matthew 18:19 where Jesus said, "*Again, truly I tell you that if two of you on earth agree about anything they ask for, it will be done for them by my Father in heaven*," and I felt that I needed a prayer partner so two of us could pray and agree together for my husband's healing. My mother was a prayer warrior and she agreed to pray with me. So, every night at nine o'clock, each of us would go to a quiet spot and lay hold of God asking that my husband would be healed and delivered from the use of the nasal spray. It was not instantaneous, but God answered our prayer! Over a period of two or three weeks, the congestion in my husband's nose went away and he no longer needed the spray in order to breathe easily through his nose. I did not tell my husband that my mother and I had been praying for this healing until he was healed. He said that he knew God had given him a miracle. For over fifty years now, my husband has not used any nasal spray. To God be the Glory!

One day when our older son was about two years old, I was on the phone talking with a friend. I heard God's still small voice speaking to me. By this, I am not talking about hearing a real audible voice but rather having a thought

19

or strong impression suddenly come to my mind. In this instance, I felt that God was saying to get off the phone and check on my son. I had no fear and no anxiety, but an urgency. So, I immediately got off the phone and went looking for my son. I found him sitting on his bedroom floor beside an overturned diaper pail. For those of you who do not know, in the days before the widespread use of disposable diapers, plastic diaper pails, or containers, were used to hold dirty diapers until they were washed. The lid to these containers usually had a small compartment that could hold a round deodorizer cake or bar. When I looked at the lid on the floor, I saw that the deodorizer bar was out of its compartment and on the floor. The bar seemed to have broken because it was missing a large piece.

I looked more closely at the remaining bar and saw small tooth marks! I immediately smelled my son's breath and, sure enough, it smelled

just like the deodorizer bar! I looked all over
the room for the missing piece and could not
find it. I knew my son had eaten it. Thank the
Lord I had saved the deodorizer box and I
began reading the label. The label stated that
the bar was a poison and, if ingested, to call
poison control. I began praying that God would
intervene and save my son. I called poison
control and told them the name of the poison
my son had eaten. I was told that the antidote
for this poison was milk—drinking as much milk
as possible. My son loved milk, but on this day
he decided he did not want any. So, I cried out
to God again and asked Him to help. As soon
as I prayed, my son began drinking the milk.
He never showed any symptoms from the
poisoning. God answered my prayers and
saved my son from everything the poison could
have done to him!

Another time my mother developed a severe
infection in her jaw and was admitted to the

hospital for treatment. While I was preparing dinner for my family, I felt a prompting to immediately stop and pray for my mother. I went to my bedroom, got on my knees, and began to pray for my mother. I felt that God said to me that my mother was dying. I started to cry and prayed that God would heal her and not let her die. The scripture from James 5:14-15 suddenly came to mind: *"Is anyone among you sick? Let them call the elders of the church to pray over them and anoint them with oil in the name of the Lord. And the prayer offered in faith will make the sick person well; the Lord will raise them up."* I told my husband, who was a deacon in our church, what had happened. He began calling the church's elders but was only able to get hold of one of them. This elder and my husband met and went to the hospital.

When they got to my mother's room, my husband said they knew that her condition was very serious. They prayed for her and anointed her with oil. I continued to pray through the night. The next morning we learned that my mother's doctor came to the hospital in the middle of the night, saw her condition, and performed an emergency surgery which saved her life! Later, the doctor told us that he could not sleep that night. So, he got up and went to the hospital just to check on my mother. Our good God answered our prayers and let my mother live. Thank you, Jesus!

Our younger son was born with a birth defect called clubfoot. In his case, both feet were rotated inwards, or almost sideways, from the normal position. Our pediatrician said that there were several treatment options, but the one he recommended was to fit our son with shoes with a metal brace attached to the bottom of each shoe. The brace was set to turn and hold his feet in the normal position and over several months the bones should grow into this position and correct the problem. The doctor said I had to keep the brace on my son's feet all the time except for five minutes a day when I washed him. After three or four months, the doctor said my son would still have to wear the brace but only at night for a year or two.

After being fitted with the shoes and brace, I began to feel so sorry for him. The brace was heavy and I knew he was uncomfortable much of the time. So, I went to my Father in Heaven and began asking for a miracle healing. Each time I took the brace off to wash his feet, I prayed and prayed. Now, I do not recommend that anyone disobey a doctor's orders, but I began taking my son's brace off for longer and longer periods of time while I prayed and massaged his feet. Two months later I took him back to the doctor for follow-up. The doctor said he did not understand it, but my son's feet looked normal and did not need any further treatment! The doctor actually complimented me on following his instructions so well! At the time, I was not brave enough to tell the doctor that God had healed my son. Instead, I just smiled and said, "Thank you, Jesus."

Sometimes God's miracles can actually include some humor. For example, when our sons were young, we often accompanied my husband when he had to travel for his work and we often carried some snacks, such as peanuts, with us when we traveled. On this particular morning, we had checked in a hotel and my husband had left for work. Suddenly, my older son ran up to me and said that his two-year-old brother had put a peanut up his nose! I looked and he really had a peanut stuck in his nose!

I got a tissue and told him to try to blow it out, but the peanut did not move. I proceeded to try to pry it out with my fingers not thinking that this was probably the worst thing I could do because I actually shoved the peanut further into his nostril. My son started crying and I began to panic. I did not know what to do. I had him to blow into a tissue again but the peanut was locked tight. I turned to God and began praying. I told God that there was no one there to help me and I needed a miracle. By faith, I took a tissue and told my son to blow once again. This time the peanut shot out like a bullet! Our good God gave us a miracle and I thanked Him for taking care of us once again.

Several years ago, my husband began suffering from plantar fasciitis which causes extreme heel pain primarily when taking the first steps after lying down or sitting. Over several months, he tried various home remedies and purchased many types of orthotic shoe inserts. He also went to a podiatrist, but nothing helped. During this time, an evangelist from Switzerland visited the Christian home group that we host each week. After speaking to our group, he asked if anyone needed prayer for healing. I immediately asked if he would pray for my husband's heel pain. The evangelist prayed a simple prayer just asking God to heal the source of my husband's pain. Well, nothing seemed to instantly happen—he still had some heel pain. But, over the course of the next two days, his pain completely disappeared and has never returned! In this case, God moved supernaturally and healed my husband but the evidence of the healing was delayed for two days.

STORIES ABOUT GOD DELIVERING FROM FEAR

Fear is a powerful emotion caused by the belief that something or someone is dangerous, likely to cause pain, or a threat. All too often fear and anxiety can take over your life, affecting your ability to eat, sleep, concentrate, travel, and enjoy everyday living. Fear of situations such as air travel or public speaking can hold you back from doing things you want or need to do.

Many scriptures speak about fear and our good God's desire that we are delivered from fear. For example, Isaiah 41:10 says, *"So do not fear, for I am with you; do not be dismayed, for I am your God"*; and Isaiah 41:13 says, *"For I am the Lord your God who takes hold of your right hand and says to you, Do not fear; I will help you."* King David said in Psalm 34:4, *"I sought the Lord, and he answered me; he delivered me from all my fears."* In John 14:27,

Jesus says, *"Peace I leave with you; my peace I give you. I do not give to you as the world gives. Do not let your hearts be troubled and do not be afraid."* And, Philippians 4:6-7 says, *"Do not be anxious about anything, but in every situation, by prayer and petition, with thanksgiving, present your requests to God. And the peace of God, which transcends all understanding, will guard your hearts and your minds in Christ Jesus."*

I was a fearful child and became a fearful adult. Even in view of all of the scriptures on not being afraid, I still had many fears. One of these was the fear of being alone at night. When my husband first started his job after college, he often traveled leaving the children and me alone at night. I knew that there was no real threat, but I was still afraid. I took the Bible with me to bed and, if I woke up during the night, I would look up and read scriptures about fear. I began to memorize many of

29

these scriptures and would quote them during the day and before I went to bed. Over a period of time, by quoting scripture, believing in His Word, and trusting in Him, God completely delivered me from the fear of being alone at night. I could then stay by myself at night with perfect confidence that God was with me and would take care of me.

A few years ago, I was alone one night and a noise woke me up. I thought I heard someone in the house. Knowing that God was with me, I got up and walked confidently through the house. The house was very dark and there were scary looking shadows everywhere. I felt that God put a simple thought in my mind—turn on a light! As soon as I switched on a light, the darkness and shadows vanished because darkness cannot stay where there is light. This was a simple reminder in the physical realm of what God does in the spiritual realm. Jesus is the light of the world. He is always with us and, where He is, darkness is driven out. I thank God we always have the light of the world at our side and I thank God for delivering me from this fear.

I do not know what caused it, but I developed a severe fear of heights as a child and I carried this fear into my adult life. When riding in a car that passed over a high bridge, I would actually close my eyes and shrink down in the seat until reaching the other side. My fear was so bad that I could not look down from a window in a multi-story building and I would avoid walking up outdoor staircases if you could see through the open space between each step. When traveling in the mountains, I missed seeing so many beautiful sights because I was afraid to look out at the scenery. For many years, this fear adversely affected many areas of my life.

One year when our sons were young, we took a trip to Southern California and planned to visit Disneyland. A day before we went to the park, we were shopping and went into a Christian bookstore. I asked God if there was a book in the store that He wanted me to read. I felt led to pick up a book about being delivered from fear. I purchased the book and read it that evening. The book ended with a prayer that you could pray to confess your fear and ask God to deliver you from it. Well, I prayed about my fear of heights and, when I did, I believed that my fear was gone. The next day we went to Disneyland. While walking in the park, I told my husband that God had delivered me from my fear of heights. He said that was wonderful and said that we should test it! He pointed up to the Disneyland Skyway ride and talked me into getting on it. I had never been on such a ride—they had always terrified me! The ride had little gondolas attached to a small wire that carried you across the park suspended high above the ground. As we waited in line for the ride, I began feeling a little uncomfortable. My anxiousness began building the closer we got.

We finally stepped into the gondola, the attendant slammed shut the door, and off we went. The gondola immediately starting rocking and I started screaming! I was so frightened and screamed to let me off the ride! But, it was too late, we were on our way to the other side of the park. I began praying as loud as I could, "Perfect love casts out fear." I prayed this loudly over and over again. About halfway into the ride, all fear suddenly vanished! Instantaneously, God answered my prayer and delivered me from my fear of heights. I started laughing and began looking down. I looked everywhere. For the first time in my life, I was high off the ground and not afraid. I was so excited that, when we got off the ride, I said to my husband, "Let's ride it again!" God had completely taken away this fear that had bound me for so many years. Our good God had done it again.

One day after returning home from a trip we noticed that our refrigerator's ice maker had stopped working. We called a repair service and they sent a man to fix the problem. When the repairman began working on the ice maker, I asked if he was a believer. He said that he was and I felt that God wanted me to share with him some of my Christian experiences and stories. After a while, he also shared some of his stories with me and I began to realize that God must have a purpose in this visit. That evening, I felt led to write the repairman a note telling him how much I was blessed by his visit.

About a week later a woman called and invited me to be the key speaker at her church's senior banquet. She said that she had attended a prayer meeting at the home of the repairman who had fixed our ice maker.

During the meeting, the repairman discussed meeting me and shared some of the experiences I had shared with him. The woman said she needed a speaker for the banquet and thought the seniors would enjoy hearing about some of my experiences. I was very surprised by the invitation. But, I remembered that just two days prior to receiving this call I felt that God was telling me my ministry outside the home was about to begin. I had told God that I would do anything He asked but that I did not want to speak before large groups. The very thought of standing before and speaking to a large group of people was very frightening to me. Yet, here I was faced with just that—an opportunity to minister but only by speaking before a group.

I told the woman I would let her know my decision the next day. As soon as we hung up, I called and told my husband about the invitation to speak. He said he believed that

God wanted me to accept the invitation even though I would have to face my fear of public speaking. I knew he was right and I called the woman back and agreed to speak. A few days before I was to speak, my fears grew. I called family and friends and asked them to pray for me. Then, I just sat before the Lord and asked Him to not let the spirit of fear overcome me nor let any symptoms of fear be manifested when I spoke. I felt that I was not capable in my own flesh to do this. But, I knew I could be a vessel and let the Lord do it through me. I also told myself that there probably would be only 10 to 15 seniors at the banquet and this really was not a very large group.

When we arrived at the church on the evening of the banquet, I noticed how many tables were set up and how many people were coming in. I asked the woman who invited me how many people was she expecting. She said about 125 to 150! Well, to me this was a very large group. Yet, in God's mercy and grace, I had no fear! When I was called up to speak, I still was not afraid and knew that God was with me. I had not prepared a speech—I just opened my mouth and relied on the Holy Spirit to give me the words to share. Afterward, my husband said I spoke for twenty-five minutes and he loved my message. God was so gracious to me. Many came up to me afterward and said they enjoyed hearing about things that God had done in my life.

The next day thoughts began to enter into my mind. I began thinking that I did a terrible job speaking at the banquet—that I said things that I should not have said and I did not say things that I should have said. Then, I stopped and realized that these thoughts were coming from the enemy and this enemy wanted to stop me from ever speaking publicly again for God. I knew that God did the speaking the night before—He just used my voice. God knew the hearts of those at the banquet and He knew what they needed to hear. By faith, I just stood in front of the people and our good God did the rest.

STORIES ABOUT GOD SUPERNATURALLY MEETING NEEDS

God cares about our needs and this caring points to His goodness. Philippians 4:19 says, *"And my God will meet all your needs according to the riches of his glory in Christ Jesus."* The stories below describe instances in my life where God showed His goodness by supernaturally answering a prayer to meet a need.

One of my early stories of God meeting a need happened when our older son was about 10 months old. One evening my husband arrived home very late after a long day at college and working at his part-time job. He was exhausted and just wanted to get some sleep. About the time he went to bed, our son, who was in his crib in the adjacent room, began to scream loudly and shake his crib for good measure. There was nothing wrong with him—he just wanted out of the crib even though it was well past his bedtime.

My husband became very frustrated and sternly said to me, "Do Something!" Well, I was tired too. It had been one of those days when our son just seemed out of control all day. So, I got angry and shouted, "God, do something!" Instantly, there was total silence. My son's screaming stopped and I could no longer hear the noise of his crib being shaken. I became frightened and my first thought was that God had killed him! Of course, this was a foolish thought, but I had never shouted at God before. I got up and went into his room. I could not believe what I saw. My son was stretched out in the crib as if someone had just tucked him into bed. He was breathing evenly like he had been sleeping for hours. I was a little shaken by this but marveled at the supernatural power of God. God understood my frustration and answered our need.

On a very hot summer day when I was pregnant with my second son, I had taken our older son outside to play. After some time, we both were very hot and wanted to get back into our house and the wonderful air conditioning. When I got to the door and tried to turn the knob, it would not move—it was locked! My husband was at work and I did not want to bother him. So, I checked our neighbors thinking that we could stay with one of them until my husband got home. But, no one was home.

I then began to pray. I asked God for a miracle, that He would open the door for me. By faith, I went back to the same door and reached for the knob. This time the knob turned and the door opened! My son and I walked into the house and enjoyed the air conditioning for the rest of the day. When my husband came home from work, I told him the story. He did not believe me and said that the door must have been unlocked the whole time. He got up to check the door and found that it was still locked tight! Our good God had met my need and supernaturally opened a locked door.

A few years later, I agreed to go door-to-door in my neighborhood to collect donations for the American Heart Association. While I was out, the clouds in the sky began to grow dark and I knew that a storm was coming. I did not have an umbrella with me and I did not want to get wet. I was a couple of blocks from home when a few drops of rain began to fall. I remembered that the Bible includes stories about God controlling the weather. So, I began to pray and ask God to hold back the rain until I completed collecting and got home. I continued to stop at each house on the way home but never got wet because the rain seemed to stay just behind me. As soon as I reached the porch of my house, the rain poured down. God had supernaturally held back the rain so I could complete my task without getting drenched!

Long ago, I volunteered as a telephone counselor at the Christian Broadcasting Network (CBN), which is headquartered in my area. CBN was having a telethon to raise money for their ministries and I agreed to help answer the phones as people called in with donations. Because I would be on the set and appear on the broadcast, I wanted to wear my nicest suit. I got all dressed up but could not find the jacket to the suit. I looked in every closet in the house and then looked a second time.

It was time to leave and I did not want to be late and miss participating in the telethon. I prayed that God would help me find the jacket. As soon as I prayed, I felt led to look once again in my younger son's room. As I walked into his room, the jacket was lying on the floor right in front of the closet door! I could hardly believe my eyes. The jacket was not there just moments ago. I knew that God had supernaturally answered my prayer. I imagined that God had dispatched an angel to place my jacket right in front of me. I was so excited! I thanked God and got to the telethon in time to answer the phones.

I went shopping one day at a small shopping center. The center was very busy and the parking spaces were very tight. I finished shopping and returned to my car. Other cars had squeezed in all around my car practically trapping me in the parking space. I was not the best of drivers and I knew that I could not pull out safely without some help. I got in the car and sat there panicking for several minutes. Finally, I did what I should have done to begin with and asked God to please send someone to help me get out of the parking space.

I looked into the rearview mirror and suddenly, and I mean suddenly, a large man appeared standing behind my car. He looked like a lumberjack because he was wearing a red plaid shirt and high boots. The man began waving at me to begin backing out of the space. I watched him in my mirror as he continued waving directions until I was out of the space. I was so relieved. I rolled down my window to thank the man for helping me. I looked where he had been standing and no one was there! I looked all around knowing that he did not have enough time to walk out of my view. But, he was gone. The man disappeared as suddenly as he appeared. I remembered Hebrews 13:2, which says, *"Do not forget to show hospitality to strangers, for by so doing some people have shown hospitality to angels without knowing it"*; and I knew that our good God had supernaturally answered my prayer by sending one of His angels to meet my need.

I have two more stories of encounters with angels. First, my husband and I were staying at a hotel outside of Washington, D.C., during one of his trips for work. One morning after he had left for work, I decided to go shopping. I remember leaving my hotel room but I do not remember much else for a period of time. I do not know what happened, but my thinking became unclear and I was confused. When my thinking began to clear, I found myself in an underground shopping center. I had no memory of entering the center and I had no idea which exit I needed to use to get back to

45

the hotel. I looked around me and there were four different ways to go. I was frightened and knew I was in trouble. I immediately cried out to Jesus for help and, as soon as I spoke His name, I felt peace. I then felt the promptings of the Holy Spirit telling me which direction to walk and then which exit to use.

Upon exiting the underground shopping center, I was in a parking area with tall buildings all around. I did not see my hotel and did not feel comfortable. Once again, I called on Jesus to help me. As soon as I did, a young man appeared and walked up to me. He had strawberry blond hair, a white shirt, and dark pants. He asked if I needed help. I felt safe with him and told him I was lost and needed directions to my hotel. He said he would walk me to the hotel. We did not speak while we were walking. After a few minutes, he stopped, pointed, and said there is your hotel. I started to walk to the hotel but turned back to thank him for his help. The young man was no longer there! He had to have been an angel sent from God to meet my need!

Second, our older son was born with a heart condition that under some conditions caused episodes of extremely fast pulse rates. Such episodes could be dangerous if left untreated. One day, I got a call from the school nurse that our son was having one of the heart episodes. I picked him up and drove to the hospital. He was given medicine and the episode stopped. Our son's doctor said he wanted to start him on a new daily medicine that should prevent the episodes from occurring. But, our son had to be admitted to the hospital for a few days so he could be monitored to ensure that the new medicine worked and there were no complications. He was admitted and I stayed with him in his room.

After a couple of days, my son was doing fine but I began to get sick. My head began hurting so badly that I could hardly move my head. I did not think I could stand the pain in my head much longer. I finally called out to God and asked Him to please send my son's doctor to the room. I was thinking that the doctor might give me something to relieve the pain. Just minutes after I prayed, my son's doctor came rushing into the room. He said a nurse, who he had never seen before, came to him and said that he was urgently needed in my son's room. The doctor was pleased to find my son was alright. The doctor looked at me, saw that I was sick, and ordered me something for my pain. He then said that my son was doing fine and could be released. I was so thankful that the medicine worked for my son and also thankful that God supernaturally moved on my behalf. I know that the nurse that the doctor had never seen was an angel sent by God.

One winter's day a couple of years ago, I went to lunch with a close friend and two of my sisters. My friend drove and after lunch she dropped us off at my house. As we entered the foyer, my husband greeted us and began helping me take off my coat. I asked him to wait a second so I could remove my wallet from my coat pocket. When I reached in the pocket, my wallet was not there! I checked the other pocket and looked on the floor but there was no wallet. I had used my wallet at the restaurant to pay for lunch and remembered that I returned it to my coat pocket because I had not taken a handbag with me.

Needless to say, I was very concerned. The wallet did not have much cash in it, but it did have my driver's license and several credit cards. My sisters and I went into our family room to sit down and my husband called my friend thinking that perhaps the wallet fell out of my coat while in her car on the way back to our house. My friend had only traveled a couple of blocks and turned around to come back to our house so she and my husband could search her car. The wallet was not in the car. Next, my husband called the restaurant and asked if a woman's wallet had been found. He was told that no wallet had been turned in.

My husband said that there was a small chance the wallet fell out of my coat and onto the parking lot when I got in my friend's car upon leaving the restaurant. He asked us where we had parked and then he drove to the restaurant. He searched the area where we had parked, found no wallet, and drove back home. While all of this was going on, I was praying. I asked God if He would perform a miracle and return the wallet to me.

When my husband walked into the family room, he told us that he did not find the wallet and would have to begin calling the credit card companies to report the lost cards. As he walked past the sofa where my older sister was sitting, he spotted something between my sister and the sofa's armrest. He stopped and said, "What's that"? My sister looked down at her side and picked up my wallet! We all were shocked and excited. The only explanation for the wallet to appear where it did was that God supernaturally returned the wallet. My husband, two sisters, and I had seen a physical miracle happen right before our eyes! I thanked God for answering my prayer and was left in awe at His goodness.

STORIES ABOUT GOD BLESSING OTHERS

Have you ever felt that God wanted you to do something that would help or bless someone else? Perhaps you have felt a prompting to say something kind to a stranger or have felt led to give money to someone you did not know. I believe that God frequently uses His people to bless others and, when He does this, it is another illustration of the goodness of God. The stories below describe times that God has used me to bless others.

One very rainy day I was standing at the sink washing dishes and thinking about God. Suddenly, this thought popped into my head. I felt that I was to stop washing the dishes, get a specific book that I had in our house, and take the book to a woman that I did not know very well. At first, I thought this could not possibly be God speaking to me because I needed to finish the dishes, the woman lived about twelve miles away, and it did not make sense to take my children out in rain just to deliver a book. But, instead of going away, the prompting got even stronger and I finally understood that this was from God. So, I found the book and got my children into the car. It poured rain all the way to the woman's house.

When I arrived, there was no car in the driveway and it appeared that no one was home. I thought, "Oh no, Lord, this was not you speaking to me." But, I felt strongly to go to the door and knock. I was surprised when the woman opened the door. She looked like she had been crying. I handed her the book. When she read the title and saw the book's subject, tears began running down her face. She said that about an hour ago she prayed and asked God for wisdom and guidance in this very area! She was so thankful. The woman and I both knew God had sent me at that exact time because of His love for her. I was so blessed to witness God's goodness in action.

For several years my husband and I taught children's church. Before we left home each Sunday, I would check to make sure we had everything we needed and also pray to ask God whether I should take anything else with us. One Sunday morning I felt God prompting me to take a particular book with me. I do not remember how I acquired the book, but it was a Christian book written for children to help explain death and what happens when people die.

We got to the church, did our normal children's church activities, and delivered the prepared lesson. When we finished, we still had a little time remaining before it was time to dismiss. I remembered the book I had picked up just before leaving our house and began to read a section of it to the children. This section of the book told about a believer who died and went to heaven. It described how wonderful heaven is.

I noticed a little four- or five-year-old boy paying close attention to every word I read. Afterward, when the boy's mother came to pick him up, I mentioned to her how interested her son was in hearing about a Christian dying and going to heaven. The mother appeared stunned. She said her son's grandmother had died a few days ago and the family had gone to the funeral. She said that her son was upset and did not understand what had happened to his grandmother. She was so grateful that I had read the book and knew that it would help her son deal with his grief. God in His goodness cared about this young boy and wanted him to know that his grandmother was having a wonderful time in heaven!

Before he retired, I often accompanied my husband when he traveled for work. While packing for these trips, I would pray and ask God if there was anything I needed to take with me to help minister to someone if given the opportunity. Preparing for a trip one day, I felt prompted to take what I called a promise book with me in order to give it to the housekeeper that cleaned our hotel room. The promise books were short booklets filled with scriptures containing many of the wonderful promises of God. I purchased these booklets, which came in regular and large print versions, in bulk and would give them to people as the Holy Spirit prompted.

On this day I felt that God was saying to take a large print promise book on the trip. When I went to get the book, I found that I had many regular print books but only one large print book. I felt hesitant about giving away the last large print book and immediately thought that hotel housekeepers usually were young women who do not need large print to read. So, I picked up a regular print promise book and put it in my bag for the trip.

We arrived at the hotel and the next morning my husband went to work. Soon there was a knock at the door and a young housekeeper came in to clean our room. I was excited because I was looking forward to giving her the promise book and telling her that Jesus loved her. With a big smile, I handed the young woman the book and said it was a gift. She took the book and looked at it. Then, she said, "Thank you, honey, but I cannot read this. I have eye problems and can only read large print books." Wow, I felt terrible—I had missed God! I told the woman that God cared for her and wanted her to have a promise book. I then told her exactly what had happened. I got her address and, as soon as we returned home, I mailed her the large print version of the book. I try to remember this story whenever I feel the Holy Spirit prompting me to do something because it is so easy to talk ourselves out of doing what God wants us to do.

Let me share three more short stories about God leading me to do something to bless others. Another time, when I was getting ready to travel with my husband, I felt led to take my anointing oil. This seemed strange to me because I could not imagine that I would encounter someone on the trip who needed to be anointed with oil. But, in obedience, I put the oil in my bag. We arrived at our destination and checked into a hotel. The next morning my husband went to work and, sometime later, the housekeeper came to clean the room. As soon as the woman entered the room, I knew that God wanted me to anoint her with oil for a ministry that she was to start. I began talking with the woman and learned that she had very recently retired from this same job. She said that she had planned to start doing ministry work for God. But, soon after retiring, she felt that God told her to go back to work at the same job because He had something for her there. The woman looked at me and said she had been waiting for me to come! I took out the oil and anointed her. I began praying that God would bless the ministry that He had for this woman. We both felt the Holy Spirit fill the room with His presence and we went to our knees before the Father! I felt so blessed that our good God had used me to anoint someone for service in His kingdom.

One morning I had gotten up early and was talking to God. As I prayed, I felt the prompting of the Holy Spirit to call a woman who went to my church and ask her if I could drive her anywhere. I did not understand this because I knew the woman had a car. Also, it was early in the morning and I did not want to disturb her. But, I believed God was speaking to me and I wanted to be obedient to His voice. So, I called the woman and asked if I could do anything for her. She said that her car had broken down and she really needed a ride to an appointment later that morning. She then told me that right before I called, she had asked God for help! I was so blessed that our good God used me to bless this woman.

Many years ago I had a friend who was going through a very dark time in her life. Her husband had died, she was in poor health, and she suffered from depression. One day, I felt that God wanted me to call her and say to her, "Jesus loves you." So, I called. My friend answered the phone and I said, "Jesus loves you." Immediately, she began to sob. I stayed on the phone, listened to her cry, and prayed silently. I felt that God did not want me to say any other words to her—just once in a while say that He loved her. After several minutes, I said goodbye and hung up.

Many times over a period of several months, God would prompt me to call my friend. Each time was exactly the same. I would only say that Jesus loved her and then listen to her cry. Months later, my friend was better. One day she called and thanked me for obeying the Holy Spirit with the phone calls. Even though I only said that Jesus loved her each time I called, she said that those words helped her make it through the darkest time in her life. God knew what my friend needed to hear and I was so blessed that He used me to deliver those powerful, life-changing words, "Jesus loves you."

STORIES ABOUT GOD'S SPECIAL BLESSINGS

God's goodness is limitless and His blessings to His people are never-ending. Because of His love for us, He desires to bless us until the blessings become overwhelming. Deuteronomy 28:2 says, *"And all these blessings shall come upon you and overtake you, if you obey the voice of the Lord your God."* (English Standard Version)   Also, James 1:17 says, *"Every good and perfect gift is from above, coming down from the Father of the heavenly lights, who does not change like shifting shadows."* I thank God for His mercies and blessings—for saving me, for my husband and family, for friends, and for health. The stories below describe some additional blessings—what I think of as special personal blessings from God that show His immeasurable goodness.

One day many years ago before CDs and MP3s, I was dusting our family room and saw a stack of vinyl record albums we owned. They were all by secular artists. I prayed and told God I would love to have Christian albums instead of the ones we had. I also mentioned this to my husband and he agreed that it would be nice to have some Christian albums, but we could not afford to purchase any. This occurred during the time that I was a volunteer telephone counselor at CBN, and the following Saturday morning I went to CBN for my scheduled shift.

CBN was broadcasting a Christian radio station at the time from their building and, as I walked in that morning, the station's disc jockey saw me and said he had something for me. I walked into his office and on his desk was a stack of Christian record albums. He said that the radio station did not need the records and wondered whether I would like to have them. I was so excited! I felt like it was Christmas. When I got home, I walked in with the albums and I told my husband what had happened. He was surprised too. He said that while I was at CBN, he had gone through our secular albums and had pulled out all but a few to give away. He looked at the stack I brought in and then looked at the stack he had gathered to give away. Then, he counted each stack. The number of secular albums he was giving away was exactly the same as the number of Christian albums that the disk jockey had given to me! God had heard my prayer and had supernaturally answered it.

Another time I was praying for God to give my husband the desires of his heart. I did not know at the time that my husband wanted to sell our house and purchase a new home. He had not mentioned it to me partly because interest rates were very high at the time and houses in our area were not selling very well. But, we began talking about it and before long we had found a new home we wanted to buy. The real problem was selling our existing house. Not only were homes in our area not selling quickly, but I had an illness at the time and was not up to showing the house to a lot of potential buyers. So, I prayed. I reminded God that He had made all of creation in six days and rested on the seventh day. Then, I asked Him if He would sell our house in seven days. I knew that I was asking for a miracle, but I had faith that God would do it.

We did not contract with a realtor to sell the house. Instead, my husband put a small ad in the newspaper and put up a "For Sale by Owner" sign in our yard. Well, not much happened over the first several days and the end of the week was approaching. Then, on the seventh day, a woman knocked on the door to our house. She said that she and her husband were moving into our area and were looking to buy a house very quickly. She looked at our house and that evening brought her husband to look at it. That night they signed a contract to purchase our house! God did it! He answered my prayer, sold our house in seven days, and gave my husband a desire of his heart! We are ordinary people, but we serve an extraordinary God!

Years ago, I went through a long-term illness before God supernaturally healed me. During this time, I listened to a lot of Christian music. I was so blessed by the music of one particular

Christian artist. I found this artist's music spoke more and more to my spirit and encouraged me by the lyrics. I loved all of the artist's songs, but there was one favorite song that just resonated within me. During this time, I prayed and asked God to please let me meet this man one day so I could personally tell him how much his music had blessed me.

A few years later after God healed me, I was invited to a conference where this man was the guest music artist. I was so excited about getting to hear him perform live. As I entered the building where the conference was held, the artist was standing there! I could hardly believe it. I introduced myself and thanked him for his music and told him what a blessing it had been in my life. Wow, God had answered my prayer from years ago! But, God's blessing did not stop there. Later that evening during the time that the artist was performing, the artist paused between songs. He said to the audience that he felt that God wanted him to sing a song that he had not planned to sing. He proceeded to sing the song. It was the one favorite song that had meant the most to me during my illness! I was amazed and so happy that God did this for me. Our good God does more than we could ever ask or think.

Let me share one final story of God's special personal blessing. It was Valentine's Day and we were having someone over for dinner. As I was setting the table a few hours before dinner, I prayed and told God that a centerpiece of red and white flowers for the table would be nice, but I did not have time to go and buy one. Later, the person coming for dinner arrived a few minutes late. When I answered the door, the person handed me a beautiful arrangement of red and white flowers! She then explained she was late because on the way to our house the thought to buy flowers for our table would not go out of her mind. So, she stopped at a florist and bought the flowers. I know that our guest brought me the flowers, but I also know that God gave them to me!

FINAL THOUGHTS

For some of you, the stories you just read might seem too incredible to be true. To this, I can only say that I have described my experiences without exaggeration. I serve an all-powerful, gracious, good God who loves to bless His people through signs, wonders, and miracles. Other readers might find the stories wonderful but believe that such things could never happen in their lives. For these readers, I want to encourage you. Remember that God has no favorites. I am just an ordinary woman saved by the grace of God. God is willing and able to answer your prayers no matter how small or how big your requests are. Live with the expectancy that our good God is ready to intervene in your life with provision, healing, deliverance, and blessings. Enjoy the journey!

SALVATION PRAYER

If you have not accepted Jesus as your Lord
and Savior but would like to do so, now is the
time. If you pray, believe, and sincerely mean
the following words, you will become born
again! God is ready to forgive all of your sins
and to welcome you into His kingdom for
eternity.

*Dear God, I know I am a sinner and I ask for
your forgiveness. I believe Jesus Christ is
Your Son. I believe that He died for my sins
and that you raised Him from the dead. I place
my trust in Him as my Savior and will follow
Him as Lord from this day forward. Please
guide my life and help me to do your will. I
pray this in the name of Jesus. Amen.*

If you just prayed and sincerely meant these
words, then welcome to God's family! The
Bible tells us to follow up on our new

commitment. You can do this by following the steps below.

1. Tell someone else about your new faith in Jesus.

2. Get water baptized.

3. Spend time with God each day by praying to Him and reading the Bible.

4. Seek fellowship with other followers of Jesus.

5. Find a Bible-believing church where you can worship God and learn more about the Kingdom of God.

71

Made in the USA
Middletown, DE
14 April 2024